AF428432

Life and Death

Faith is the Difference

TABLE OF CONTENTS

In this world there are really only 2 major aspects. Life and Death. There is no middle crossroad.

Proverbs 18:21 Death and life are in the power of the tongue: and they that love it shall eat the fruit thereof.

Hebrews 11:1-3

1 Now faith is the substance of things hoped for, the evidence of things not seen.

2 For by it the elders obtained a good report.

3 Through faith we understand that the worlds were framed by the word of God, so that things which are seen were not made of things which do appear.

As Christians we are always dealing with two issues, life and death. As we go through life there comes a point when everything ends and we will have made one of two decisions accept

Christ or not. That is where faith comes in, this book will discuss faith and how faith works to help us decide which way we will choose in life.

Deuteronomy 30:19 I call heaven and earth to record this day against you, that I have set before you life and death, blessing and cursing: therefore choose life, that both thou and thy seed may live:

We have the choice how we want to live life by making the right choice and saying the right things. Each and every day there are many choices that we make, some good, some not so good, some totally bad. The way we handle these choices will determine the outcome of our future.

As life begins as a child, the child is trained to believe – or have faith in – their parents. As the child grows up, they have to make a personal choice to either live for Christ or for the world.

Hebrews 11:1-3

1 Now faith is the substance of things hoped for, the evidence of things not seen.

2 For by it the elders obtained a good report.

3 Through faith we understand that the worlds were framed by the word of God, so that things which are seen were not made of things which do appear.

Proverbs 18:21

Death and life are in the power of the tongue: and they that love it shall eat the fruit thereof.

Deuteronomy 30:19

I call heaven and earth to record this day against you, that I have set before you life and death, blessing and cursing: therefore choose life, that both thou and thy seed may live:

Revelation 3:15-16 NLT

[15] "I know all the things you do, that you are neither hot nor cold. I wish that you were one or the other!

[16] But since you are like lukewarm water, neither hot nor cold, I will spit you out of my mouth!

We have the choice how we want to live life by making the right choice and saying the right things.

Each and every day there are many choices that we make, some good, some not so good, some totally bad. The way we handle these choices will determine the outcome of our future.

2 Corinthians 4:13

13 It is written: "I believed; therefore I have spoken." Since we have that same spirit of faith, we also believe and therefore speak,

Decision time

John 3: 15-16, 36

15 That whosoever believeth in him should not perish, but have eternal life.

16 For God so loved the world, that he gave his only begotten Son, that whosoever believeth in him should not perish, but have everlasting life.

36 He that believeth on the Son hath everlasting life: and he that believeth not the Son shall not see life; but the wrath of God abideth on him.

John 5:2-9

Like the man at the pool of Bethesda, we must believe on Christ to have eternal life. That requires faith.

Romans 10:17

17 So then faith cometh by hearing, and hearing by the word of God.

We have to hear about something before we can trust in it. You cannot make a decision to accept Christ without first hearing about Him. Once you hear, then you have to believe it is true. That takes faith.

Hosea 4:6

6 My people are destroyed for lack of knowledge: because thou hast rejected knowledge, I will also reject thee, that thou shalt be no priest to me: seeing thou hast forgotten the law of thy God, I will also forget thy children.

It requires knowledge to build faith.

Romans 12:2-3

2 And be not conformed to this world: but be ye transformed by the renewing of your mind, that ye may prove what is that good, and acceptable, and perfect, will of God.

3 For I say, through the grace given unto me, to every man that is among you, not to think of himself more highly than he ought to think; but to think soberly, according as God hath dealt to every man the measure of faith.

God has given every man a measure of faith. When we present the Word to people, it is this measure that the person has to depend on if they are being told the truth or not.

What are you going to give your time to, God, or the world?

Action Time

Faith is real. It doesn't matter if you believe in God or not you are still using FAITH. Faith is believing something without real proof that it even exists. You use faith in everything you expect or hope for.

Faith is believing in something because you spend time focusing on it. Give God time and He will strengthen your faith in Him. Give the world time and your faith in it will strengthen also.

Hebrews 11:1

1 Now faith is the substance of things hoped for, the evidence of things not seen.

Romans 10:17

17 So then faith cometh by hearing, and hearing by the word of God.

Believing Faith

BELIEVE, verb transitive To credit upon the authority or testimony of another; to be persuaded of the truth of something upon the declaration of another, or upon evidence furnished by reasons, arguments, and deductions of the mind, or by other circumstances, than personal knowledge.

There are times that all we can do is stand and believe. God can only help if we learn to " get self out of the way." That is not always easy to do since we like to be involved in what happens with our life. We want to be the one that decides how things happen and fall into place. If we take the time to listen to God, He will give us all the information and resources to make the right choices. Once we listen to Him then we will know how to proceed and follow His will for our lives.

We will always hear a lot of different opinions, but it matters what we believe. Do we believe what those around us are saying or do we believe God's Word and listen to what God is trying to tell us.

Romans 4:17-18

[17] (As it is written, I have made thee a father of many nations,) before him whom he believed, even God, who quickeneth the dead, and calleth those things which be not as though they were.

[18] Who against hope believed in hope, that he might become the father of many nations, according to that which was spoken, So shall thy seed be.

Matthew 21:22

[22] And all things, whatsoever ye shall ask in prayer, believing, ye shall receive.

When we take time to get into God's word and really pay attention to it, we will start talking and saying it all the time(abide). The only way God is going to answer every prayer is if we are asking and believing according to His word.   You can quote scripture all day long but if you are not mixing it with believing faith, it will not come to pass.

John 15:7

[7] If ye abide in me, and my words abide in you, ye shall ask what ye will, and it shall be done unto you.

Hebrews 11:6

[6] But without faith it is impossible to please him: for he that cometh to God must believe that he is, and that he is a rewarder of them that diligently seek him.

Things you are believing for

Giving Faith

Giving is a very important aspect of our Christian walk. We must not only think about money but everything that we do or say. Any action you take or words that come out of your mouth, you are giving. Any time you give something, and you are expecting a harvest, it requires faith. Are you giving because you are supposed to or are you planting a seed expecting a harvest.

Luke 6:38

[38] Give, and it shall be given unto you; good measure, pressed down, and shaken together, and running over, shall men give into your bosom. For with the same measure that ye mete withal it shall be measured to you again.

2 Corinthians 9:6-8

[6] But this I say, He which soweth sparingly shall reap also sparingly; and he which soweth bountifully shall reap also bountifully.

[7] Every man according as he purposeth in his heart, so let him give; not grudgingly, or of necessity: for God loveth a cheerful giver.

[8] And God is able to make all grace abound toward you; that ye, always having all sufficiency in all things, may abound to every good work:

Matthew 6:33

³³ But seek ye first the kingdom of God, and his righteousness; and all these things shall be added unto you.

Malachi 3:10

¹⁰ Bring ye all the tithes into the storehouse, that there may be meat in mine house, and prove me now herewith, saith the Lord of hosts, if I will not open you the windows of heaven, and pour you out a blessing, that there shall not be room enough to receive it.

1 Timothy 6:10

¹⁰ For the love of money is the root of all evil: which while some coveted after, they have erred from the faith, and pierced themselves through with many sorrows.

Money and possessions are not the end all be all. They are tools, to be used to push forward the Kingdom of God in this world. We have to learn how to mix faith with our giving in order to receive and not just give because we are supposed to. This is a principle of faith that is overlooked by too many people. It requires faith with our giving in order to receive any blessing from that giving.

Things you are giving towards

Healing Faith

We all face sickness and disease in our lives. It matters how we face those issues. We can just try to cope with it and think maybe it will pass. That is what the devil wants. That way he can defeat us and keep us from achieving what we were called to do. As Christians, we have to put our faith in the word and claim our healings. Even if the healings don't manifest immediately, we still have to stand on the word and use our faith to overcome the issues.

Isaiah 53:5

5 But he was wounded for our transgressions, he was bruised for our iniquities: the chastisement of our peace was upon him; and with his stripes we are healed.

1 Peter 2:24

24 Who his own self bore our sins in his own body on the tree, that we, being dead to sins, should live unto righteousness: by whose stripes ye were healed.

Healing is something that we all need from time to time. We have to learn how to mix faith with healing scriptures and prayers in order to receive any healing from God.

Malachi 4:2

But unto you that fear my name shall the Sun of righteousness arise with healing in his wings; and ye shall go forth and grow up as calves of the stall.

Jeremiah 17:14

14 Heal me, O Lord, and I shall be healed; save me, and I shall be saved: for thou art my praise.

The only way we are going to receive any healing from God, is we have to declare the healing according to His word and mix our faith with our declarations. If we declare God's word back to Him in faith, He has no choice but to respond.

Isaiah 55:8-11

8 For my thoughts are not your thoughts, neither are your ways my ways, saith the Lord.

9 For as the heavens are higher than the earth, so are my ways higher than your ways, and my thoughts than your thoughts.

10 For as the rain cometh down, and the snow from heaven, and returneth not thither, but watereth the earth, and maketh it bring forth and bud, that it may give seed to the sower, and bread to the eater:

11 So shall my word be that goeth forth out of my mouth: it shall not return unto me void, but it shall accomplish that which I please, and it shall prosper in the thing whereto I sent it.

Healings you are believing for

Trusting Faith

Proverbs 3:5-6

5 Trust in the Lord with all thine heart; and lean not unto thine own understanding.

6 In all thy ways acknowledge him, and he shall direct thy paths.

Everyday situations require some type of trust. You are either trusting God, yourself, or someone else to get through it. We as Christians must learn to depend on the guidance of the Holy Spirit to get the best result in the situation.

Psalms 118:8

8 It is better to trust in the Lord than to put confidence in man.

We must always remember that there are certain people we can turn to for wisdom and understanding.

Proverbs 19:20

20 Hear counsel, and receive instruction, that thou mayest be wise in thy latter end.

Things you are trusting God for

23

Standing Faith

Hebrews 3:14 NLT

14 For if we are faithful to the end, trusting God just as firmly as when we first believed, we will share in all that belongs to Christ.

Ephesians 6:10-18

10 Finally, my brethren, be strong in the Lord, and in the power of his might.

11 Put on the whole armour of God, that ye may be able to stand against the wiles of the devil.

12 For we wrestle not against flesh and blood, but against principalities, against powers, against the rulers of the darkness of this world, against spiritual wickedness in high places.

13 Wherefore take unto you the whole armour of God, that ye may be able to withstand in the evil day, and having done all, to stand.

14 Stand therefore, having your loins girt about with truth, and having on the breastplate of righteousness.

15 And your feet shod with the preparation of the gospel of peace.

16 Above all, taking the shield of faith, wherewith ye shall be able to quench all the fiery darts of the wicked.

17 And take the helmet of salvation, and the sword of the Spirit, which is the word of God:

18 Praying always with all prayer and supplication in the Spirit and watching thereunto with all perseverance and supplication for all saints.

There will be battles in all our lives. We will be faced with situations where in our natural mind, we do not know what to do. We have to remember where the battle is coming from. We have to recognize the power we have in the blood of Christ and use that power in biblical declarations against the enemy.

1 Peter 1:19-21

19 But with the precious blood of Christ, as of a lamb without blemish and without spot:

20 Who verily was foreordained before the foundation of the world, but was manifest in these last times for you,

21 Who by him do believe in God, that raised him up from the dead, and gave him glory; that your faith and hope might be in God.

Things you are standing in faith for

Reward Time

Life gives us plenty of opportunities to use faith. If you will apply the concepts explained in this book, then you can and will live a successful Christian life. It will require some consistent behaviors, but it does work. Faith will work in your life in every situation. Remember Faith is the substance of things hoped for, the evidence of things not seen. If you are asking God for something but in your heart you don't believe it will happen, then it will not happen. We have to believe that we will receive what we are asking for before it even has a chance of coming to pass.

1 John 5:4 AMP

For everyone born of God is victorious and overcomes the world; and this is the victory that has conquered and overcome the world—our [continuing, persistent] faith [in Jesus the Son of God].

Revelation 21:8

But the cowardly, the unbelieving, the vile, the murderers, the sexually immoral, those who

practice magic arts, the idolaters and all liars-
their place will be in the fiery lake of burning
sulfur. This is the second death."

31